THE BEST
OF THE WORST

DAD JOKES

OVER *100* JOKES!

PUNNY
PUBLISHING

ISBN-10: 1976077451

ISBN-13: 978-1976077456

WHAT'S THE RESEMBLANCE BETWEEN A GREEN APPLE AND A RED APPLE?

THEY'RE BOTH RED.. EXCEPT FOR THE GREEN ONE!

MY WIFE DIDN'T LAUGH AT ANY OF MY JOKES WHILE SHE WAS IN LABOUR!

IT MUST HAVE BEEN THE DELIVERY!

I JUST DON'T UNDERSTAND WHY THE GOVERNMENT WOULD HIRE A POLITE SNAKE?

MAYBE IT'S BECAUSE HE'S A CIVIL SERPENT!

I'M SO PROUD TO HAVE FINALLY FINISHED THE PUZZLE I STARTED 12 MONTHS AGO..

THE BOX SAID IT WOULD TAKE 3-5 YEARS!

DAD, WHY WON'T YOU LET ME HAVE A POTATO GUN?

BECAUSE IT'S A WEAPON OF MASH DESTRUCTION!

53

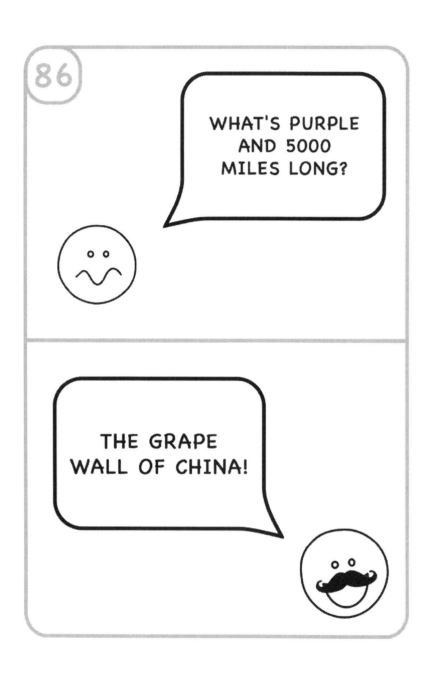

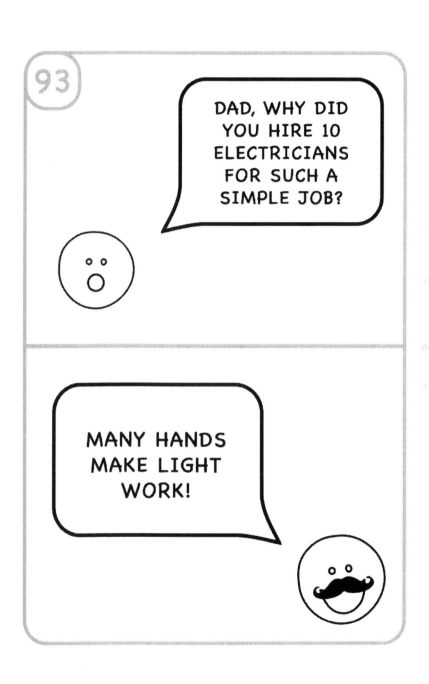

100
YOU MISSED WORK YESTERDAY, DIDN'T YOU!?
NOT REALLY!

WHAT ARE YOU GOING TO DO ABOUT YOUR FEAR OF ELEVATORS?

I'M GOING TO START TAKING STEPS TO AVOID THEM

Thank You

I really hope you've enjoyed this book and had a good laugh at the awful Dad Jokes!

Please leave a review on **Amazon** if you have the time!

Thanks again!

23843640R00066

Printed in Great Britain
by Amazon